Presented to:

_____

_____

By:

_____

_____

_____ 19_____

Brownlow Gift Books

The University of Hard Knocks

THE SCHOOL THAT COMPLETES YOUR EDUCATION

BY RALPH PARLETTE

BROWNLOW PUBLISHING COMPANY, INC.

Brownlow Publishing Company, Inc.
6309 Airport Freeway, Fort Worth, Texas 76117

· CONTENTS ·

In the Dim, Distant Past, some shade-tree philosopher made the observation that one picture is worth ten thousand words. Since that time, countless others have quoted the original in one form or another. From my perspective, the individual who says—and believes—that statement has never read the Declaration of Independence or the Bill of Rights. They've certainly never read the 23rd Psalm nor have they prayed the Lord's Prayer or read and understood John 3:16. All of those are words—just words—but those words have changed the course of history and affected the lives of untold millions of people.

The University of Hard Knocks is approximately fifteen thousand words, but it is my firm belief that these words are also destined to affect the lives of a tremendous number of people. The author has put these words together in a beautiful series of lessons which encourage on occasion, chastise very gently on other occasions, poke a little fun at us on yet additional occasions, but always with gentle love wrapped around considerable optimism designed to raise our hopes because of the very practicality and believability of what he is saying. Charles Osgood was "right on" when he said, "Compared to the spoken word, a picture is a pitiful thing indeed."

The University of Hard Knocks is a book which you can pick up and read a paragraph with the thought that you're going to get a mental or spiritual "snack," only to discover that on a single page you can get a magnificent feast which will set your own mind and imagination in gear and send your hopes and optimism soaring. I encourage you to pick this little gem up and race through it as quickly as possible, to get a concept of the philosophy involved. Then I encourage you to get your pen and highlight the messages which are most meaningful to you. Read and mark slowly and deliberately, making notes in the margins as you go, so you can really get the many beautiful messages which can make a difference in your life. Here's a little book which you will get a lot out of, but which will get infinitely more out of you.

Zig Ziglar

CHAPTER ONE

The Greatest School

THE GREATEST SCHOOL is the University of Hard Knocks. Its books are bumps.

Every bump is a lesson. If we learn the lesson with one bump, we do not get that bump again. We do not need it. We have traveled beyond it. They do not waste the bumps. We get promoted to the next bump.

Some of us learn to go forward with a few bumps, but most of us are "naturally bright" and have to be pulverized.

The tuition in the University of Hard Knocks is not free. Experience is the dearest teacher in the world. Most of us spend our lives in the A-B-C's of getting started.

We matriculate in the cradle.

We never graduate. When we stop learning we are due for another bump.

There are two kinds of people—wise people and fools. The fools are the people who think they have graduated.

The playground is all of God's universe.

The university colors are black and blue.

The school yell is "ouch" repeated ad lib.

The Need for Bumps

When I was thirteen I knew a great deal more than I do now. There was a sentence in my English book that disgusted me. It was by some foreigner I had never met. His name was Shakespeare. It was this:

Sweet are the uses of adversity;
Which, like the toad, ugly and venomous,
Wears yet a priceless jewel in its head;
And thus our life, exempt from public haunt,
Finds tongues in trees, books in running brooks,
Sermons in stones, and good in everything.

"Tongues in trees," I thought. "Trees can't talk! Books in running brooks! Why no one puts books in running brooks. They'd get wet. And that sermons in stones! They get preachers to preach sermons, and they build houses out of stones."

I was sorry for Shakespeare—when I was thirteen.

There are two kinds
of people—wise
people and fools.
The fools are
the people who
think they have
graduated.

But I am happy today that I have traveled a little farther. I am happy that I have begun to learn the lessons from the bumps. I am happy that I am learning the sweet though painful lessons of the University of Adversity. I am happy that I am beginning to listen. For as I learn to listen, I hear every tree speaking, every stone preaching and in every running brook the unfolding of a book.

I was not interested when my parents told me these things. I knew they meant well, but the world had moved since they were young, and now two and two made seven, because we lived so much faster.

It is hard to tell some young people anything. They know better. So they have to get bumped just where we got bumped, to learn that two and two always makes four, and "whatsoever a man soweth, that shall he also reap."

The Two Colleges

As we get bumped and battered on life's pathway, we discover we get two kinds of bumps—bumps that we need and bumps that we do not need.

Bumps that we bump into and bumps that bump into us.

We discover, in other words, that The University of Hard Knocks has two colleges—The College of Needless Knocks and The College of Needful Knocks.

We attend both colleges.

CHAPTER TWO

The College of Needless Knocks

NEARLY ALL THE BUMPS we get are Needless Knocks. There comes a vivid memory of one of my early Needless Knocks as I say that. It was during the time when I was trying to run our home to suit myself. I sat in the highest chair in the family circle. I was three years old and ready to graduate.

That day they had the little joy and sunshine of the family in his highchair throne right beside the table. The coffeepot was within grabbing distance.

I became enamored with that coffeepot. I decided I needed that coffeepot in my business. I reached over to get the coffeepot. Then I discovered a woman beside me, my mother. She was the most meddlesome woman I had ever known. I had not tried to do one thing in three years that that woman had not meddled into.

And that day when I wanted the coffeepot—I did want it. No one knows how I desired it.

As I was reaching over to get it, that woman said, "Don't touch that!"

The longer I thought about it the more angry I became. What right has that woman to meddle into my affairs all the time? I have stood this petticoat tyranny three years, and it is time to stop it!

I stopped it. I got the coffeepot. I know I got it. I know when I got it and I also know where I got it. I got about a gallon of the hottest coffee a bad boy ever spilled over himself.

I can feel it yet!

There were weeks after that when I was upholstered. They put applebutter on me—and coal oil and white-of-an-egg and starch and anything else the neighbors could think of. They would bring it over and rub it on the little joy and sunshine of the family, who had been temporarily eclipsed.

The Coffeepots of Life

You see, my mother's way was to tell me and then let me do as I pleased. She told me not to get the coffeepot and then let me get it, knowing that it would burn me. She would say, "Don't." Then she would go on with her knitting and let me do as I pleased.

Why don't mothers knit today?

"I can do wrong and not get bumped. I have no feelings upon the subject," someone says. You can? You poor old sinner, you have bumped your conscience numb. That is why you have no feelings on the subject. You have pounded your soul into jelly. You don't know how badly you are hurt.

How the old devil works day and night to keep people amused and doped so that they will not think upon their ways! How he keeps the music and the dazzle going so they will not see they are bumping themselves!

CHAPTER THREE

The College of Needful Knocks

BUT OCCASIONALLY ALL OF US get bumps that we do not bump into. They bump into us. They are the guideboard knocks that point us to the higher pathway.

The Bumps That Bump Into Us

You were bumped yesterday or years ago. Maybe the wound has not yet healed. Maybe you think it never will heal. You wondered why you were bumped. Some of you are still wondering why.

You were doing right—doing just the best you knew how—and yet some blow came crushing down upon you and gave you cruel pain.

It broke your heart. You have had your heart broken. I have had my heart broken more times than I care to talk about now. Your home was darkened, your plans were wrecked, you thought you had nothing more to live for.

*I am like you.
I have had more
trouble than anyone
else. I have never
known anyone who
has not had more
trouble than
anyone else.*

I am like you. I have had more trouble than anyone else. I have never known anyone who has not had more trouble than anyone else.

But I am discovering that life only gets good after we have been hurt a few times.

We all must learn, if we have not already learned, that these blows are lessons in The College of Needful Knocks. They point upward to a higher path than we have been traveling.

In other words, we are raw material. You know what raw material is—material that needs more Needful Knocks to make it more useful and valuable.

The clothing we wear, the food we eat, the house we live in, all must have Needful Knocks to become useful. And so does humanity need the same preparation for greater usefulness.

The people I appreciate the most are the ones who have known more of these knocks—who have faced the great crises of life and have been tried in the crucibles of affliction. For I am learning that these lives are the gold tried in the fire.

Sufferings of the Red Mud

Years ago, I was in northern Minnesota and came to a hole in the ground. It was a big hole—about a half-mile of hole. There were shovels at work throwing out of that hole what I thought was red mud.

"Sir, why are they throwing that red mud out of that hole?" I asked a native.

"It's not red mud. It's iron ore. It's not worth anything here; that's why they're moving it away."

There's red mud around every community that is not worth anything until you move it—send it to college or somewhere.

Not very long after this, in Pennsylvania, I saw some of this same red mud. It had been moved over the Great Lakes to a blast furnace, the technological name for The College of Needful Knocks for Red Mud.

I watched this red mud matriculate into a great hopper with limestone, charcoal and other "textbooks." Then they corked it up and school began. They roasted it. It is a great thing to be roasted.

When it was finished roasting they stopped. Have you noticed that they always stop when anything is finished roasting? If we are still being roasted, perhaps we are not done!

Then they pulled the plug out of the bottom of the college and held promotion exercises. The red mud squirted out into the sand. It was not red mud now, because it had been roasted. It was a freshman— pig iron, worth more than red mud, because it had been roasted.

Some of the pig iron moved into another department, a big teakettle, where it was again roasted, and now it came out a sophomore—steel, worth more than pig iron.

Some of the sophomore steel moved up into another grade where it was roasted again and rolled thin into a junior. Some of the steel moved on up and up, at every step getting more pounding and roasting and affliction.

It seemed as though I could hear the suffering red mud crying out, "O, why did they take me away from my happy hole-in-the-ground? Why do they pound me and break my heart? I have been good and faithful. O, why do they roast me? O, I'll never get over this!"

But after they had given it a diploma—a price tag telling how much it had been roasted—they took it proudly all over the world, labeled "Made in America." They hung it in show windows, they put it in glass cases. Many people admired it and said, "Isn't that fine work!" They paid much money for it now. They paid the most money for what had been roasted the most.

You and I are the raw material, the green trees, the red mud. The Needful Knocks are necessary to make us serviceable.

Every bump is raising our price. Every bump is disclosing a path to a larger life. The diamond and the chunk of soft coal are exactly the same material, say the chemists. But the diamond has gone to The College of Needful Knocks more than has her crude sister.

There is no human diamond that has not been crystallized in the crucibles of affliction. There is no gold that has not been refined in the fire.

Lessons from the Bumps

One evening as I was speaking, a handicapped woman was wheeled down to the front of the audience. The subject was The University of Hard Knocks. Presently the woman's face was shining brighter than the footlights.

She knew about the knocks!

Afterwards I spoke to her. "I want to thank you for coming here. I have the feeling that I spoke the words, but you are the lecture itself."

What a smile she gave me! "Yes, I know about the hard knocks," she said. "I have been in pain most of my life. But I have learned all that I know sitting in this chair. I have learned to be patient and kind and loving and brave."

They told me this woman was the sweetest-spirited, best-loved person in the town.

But her mother petulantly interrupted me. She had wheeled the woman to the front. She was tall and stately and well dressed. She lived in one of the finest homes in the city. She had everything that money could buy. But her money seemed unable to buy the frown from her face.

"Mr. Parlette," she said, "why is everyone interested in my daughter and no one interested in me? Why is my daughter happy and why am I not? My daughter is always happy and she hasn't a single thing to make her happy. I am not happy. I have not been for years. Why am I not happy?"

What would you have said? Just on the spur of the moment, I said, "Madam, I don't want to be unkind, but I really think the reason you are not happy is that you haven't been bumped enough."

The handicapped girl had traveled ahead of her jealous mother. For selfishness cripples us more than paralysis.

When I visit the hospital, I want to congratulate the patients lying there. They are learning the precious lessons of patience, sympathy, love, faith and courage. They are getting the education in the humanities the world needs more than poetry or math. Only those who have suffered can sympathize. They are to become a precious part of our population. The world needs them more than libraries and foundations.

The Silver Lining

There is no backward step in life. All our experiences are truly new chapters in our education if we are willing to learn them.

We think this is true of the good things that come to us, but we do not want to think so of the bad things. Yet we grow more in lean years than in fat years. In fat years we put it in our pockets. In lean years we put it in our hearts. Material and spiritual prosperity do not often travel hand-in-hand. When we become materially very prosperous, so many of us begin to say, "Is not this Babylon that I have builded?" And about that time some handwriting appears on the wall and a bump to save us.

Think of what might happen to you today. Your home might burn. We don't want your home to burn, but someone's home is burning just now. Or fire might sweep your town from the map. Your business might wreck. Your fortune might be swept away. Your good name might be tarnished. Bereavement might take from you the one you love most.

You would never know how many real friends you have until then. But look out! Some of your friends would say, "I am so sorry for you. You are down and out." Do not believe that you are down and out, for it is not true. The old enemy of humanity wants you to believe you are down and out. He wants you to sympathize with yourself. You are never down and out!

The truth is, another chapter of your real education has been opened. Will you read the lesson of the Needful Knocks?

A great fire, a tornado, an epidemic or other public disaster brings sympathy, bravery, brotherhood and love in its wake.

There is a silver lining to every hard knocks cloud.

CHAPTER FOUR

Shake the Barrel

N OW AS WE LEARN the lessons of the Needless and the Needful Knocks, we get wisdom, understanding, happiness, strength, success and greatness. We go up in life. We become educated. Let me tell you a story about it.

The Big Apples

As a boy, I hauled a wagon full of apples to the cider-mill over a terribly rough road. As I traveled, apples sorted out by the jolting. The big apples rose to the top. The little, runty apples began holding a mass meeting at the bottom.

I saw that for thirty years before I saw it. Did you ever notice how long you have to see most things before you see them? I saw that when I played marbles. The big marbles would shake to the top of my pocket and the little ones would rattle down to the bottom.

Do not wait thirty years to learn that the big ones shake up and the little ones shake down. Put some big ones and some little things of about the same density in a box or other container and shake them. You will see the larger things shake upward and the smaller shake downward. You will see every single thing shake to the place its size determines.

Mix them up again and shake. Watch them all shake back as they were before, the largest on top and the smallest at the bottom.

When things find their place, you can shake on until doomsday, but you cannot change the place of one of the objects.

The same law that shakes the little ones down and the big ones up in that can is shaking every person to the place he fits in the barrel of life. It is sending small people down and great people up.

And do you not see that we are very foolish when we want to be lifted up to some big place, or when we want some big person to be put down to some little place? We are foolishly trying to overturn the eternal law of life.

We shake right back to the place our size determines. We must get ready for places before we can get them and keep them.

The very worst thing that can happen to anyone is to be artificially boosted up into some place where he rattles.

Kings and Queens of Destiny

The objects in that box cannot change their size. But thank God, you and I are not helpless victims of blind fate. We are not creatures of chance. We have it in our hands to decide our destiny as we grow or refuse to grow.

If we wish to change our place, we must first change our size. If we wish to go down, we must grow smaller and we shall shake down. If we wish to go up, we must grow greater, and we shall shake up.

Each person is doing one of three things consciously or unconsciously.

1. He is holding his place.
2. He is going down.
3. He is going up.

In order to hold his place he must hold his size. He must fill the place. If he shrinks up he will rattle. No one can stay long where he rattles. Nature abhors a rattler. He shakes down to a smaller place.

The "Green," Dutch Girl

So everywhere you look you see the barrel sorting people according to size. Every business organization has had this same experience. Some young women had been working in an office for a long time. There came a "green" Dutch girl from the country. It was her first office experience, and she got the lowest job.

The other girls poked fun at her and played jokes upon her because she was so green.

Do you remember that green things grow?

"Is she something else?" they said as they nudged one another. She was. She made many blunders. But she never made the same mistake twice. She learned the lesson with one helping to the bumps.

And she never "got done." When she had finished her work, she would discover something else that ought to be done, and go right on working, contrary to the rules. She had that rare quality the world is searching for—initiative.

The other girls "got done." When they had finished the work they had been assigned, they would wait— O, so patiently they would wait—to be told what to do next.

Within three months every other girl in the office was asking questions of the little Dutch girl. She had learned more about business in three months than the others had learned in years. Nothing ever escaped her. She had become the most capable girl in the office.

The barrel did the rest. Today she is giving orders to all of them, for she is the office manager.

The other girls were hurt about it. They will tell you in confidence that it was the rankest favoritism ever known. "There was nothing fair about it. Jennie should have been made manager. Jennie has been here four years."

Life's Leveler

So books could be filled with similar stories of how people have gone up and down. You may have noticed two brothers start with the same chance, and presently notice that one is going up and the other is going down.

Some of us begin life on the top branches, right in the sunshine of popular favor, and get our names in the blue-book at the start. Some of us begin down in the shade on the bottom branches, and we do not even get invited. We often become discouraged as we look at the top-branchers, and we say, "O, if I only had his chance! If I were only up there I might amount to something. But I am too low down."

We can grow. Everyone can grow.

We are all in the barrel of life, shaken and bumped about. There the real people do not often ask us, "On what branch of that tree did you grow?" But they often inquire, "Are you big enough to fill this place?"

CHAPTER FIVE

Ready to Receive

YOUNG PEOPLE COME into life wanting great places. I would not give much for a young person (or any other person) who does not want a great place. I would not give much for anyone who does not look forward to greater and better things tomorrow.

We often think the way to get a great place is just to go after it and get it. If we do not have pull enough, get some more pull. Get some more testimonials.

We think if we could only get into a great place we would be great. But unless we have grown as great as the place we would be a great joke, for we would rattle. And when we have grown as great as the place, that sized place will generally come seeking us.

We must get ready
for things before
we get them.
All life is
preparation for
greater things.

We do not become great by getting into a great place, any more than a boy becomes a man by getting into his father's boots. He is in great boots, but he rattles. He must grow greater feet before he gets greater boots.

We must get ready for things before we get them.

All life is preparation for greater things.

Moses was eighty years getting ready to do forty years work. The Master was thirty years getting ready to do three years work. Too many of us expect to get ready in "four easy lessons."

We can be a pumpkin in one summer. We can be a mushroom in a day. But we cannot become an oak that way.

Fix People, Not the Barrel

There are so many loving, sincere, foolish, cruel uplifting movements in the land. They spring up, fail, wail, disappear, only to be succeeded by twice as many more. They fail because instead of having the barrel do the uplifting, they try to do it with a crane.

The victims of the artificial lift cannot stay uplifted. They rattle back, and "the last estate of that man is worse than the first."

You cannot lift up a beggar by giving him alms. You are using the crane. We must feed the hungry and clothe the naked, but that is not helping them, that is propping them up. The beggar who asks you to help him does not want to be helped. He wants to be propped up. He wants you to license him and professionalize him as a beggar.

You can only help a man to help himself. Help him to grow. You cannot help many people, for there are not many people willing to be helped on the inside. Not many willing to grow up.

I used to say, "No one understands my talent. No one gives me a chance." But if chances had been snakes, I would have been bitten a hundred times a day. We need optometrists, not more opportunities.

I used to work on the railroad and get a dollar and fifteen cents a day. I did not earn my dollar fifteen. I tried to see how little I could do and look like I was working. I was the Artful Dodger of Section Sixteen. When the whistle would blow—O, joyful sound!—I would leave my pick hanging right up in the air. I would not bring it down again for a soulless corporation.

I used to wonder as I passed the bank on the way down to the railroad why was I not president of the bank. I wondered why I was not sitting upon one of those mahogany seats instead of pumping a hand-car. I was naturally bright. I used to say, "If the rich weren't getting richer and the poor poorer, I'd be president of a bank."

I am so glad now that I did not get to be president

of the bank. They are glad, too! I would have rattled down in about fifteen minutes, down to the peanut row, for I was only a peanut. Remember, the hand-car job is just as honorable as the bank job, but because I was not faithful over a few things, I would have rattled over many things.

The fairy tales love to tell about some clodhopper suddenly enchanted into a king. But in life, the clodhopper is enchanted into readiness for kingship before he lands upon the throne. The only way to rule others is to learn to rule ourself.

I used to say, "Just wait until I get to Congress." I think they are all waiting! "I'll fix things. I'll pass laws requiring all apples to be the same size. Yes, I'll pass laws to turn the barrel upside down, so the little ones will be on the top and the big ones will be at the bottom."

But I had not seen that it wouldn't matter which end was the top, the big ones would shake right up to it and the little ones would shake down to the bottom.

The little man has the chance now, just as fast as he grows. You cannot fix the barrel. You can only fix the people inside the barrel.

Have you ever noticed that the man who is not willing to fix himself, is the one who wants to get the most laws passed to fix other people? He wants something for nothing.

Cruel Fate

O, I am so glad I did not get the things I wanted at the time I wanted them! They would have been coffee-pots. Thank goodness, we do not get the coffee pot until we are ready to handle it.

Today you and I have things we couldn't have yesterday. We just wanted them yesterday. O, how we wanted them! But a cruel fate would not let us have them. Today we have them. They come to us naturally today because we have grown ready for them, and the barrel has shaken us up to them.

Today you and I want things beyond our reach. O, how we want them! But a cruel fate will not let us have them.

Do you not see that "cruel fate" is our own smallness and unreadiness? As we grow greater we have greater things. We have today all we can stand today. More would wreck us. More would start us to rattling.

Getting up is growing up.

And this blessed old barrel of life is just waiting and anxious to shake everyone up as fast as we are ready to receive.

CHAPTER SIX

The Secret of Greatness

WE GO UP as we grow great. That is, we go up as we grow up. But so many are trying to grow great on the outside without growing great on the inside.

They fool themselves, but no one else.

There is only one greatness—inside greatness.

All outside greatness is merely an incidental reflection of the inside.

Greatness is not measured in any material terms. It is not measured in inches, dollars, acres, votes, praises, or by any other of the world's yardsticks or barometers.

True Greatness

Greatness is measured in spiritual terms. It is education. It is life expansion.

We go up from selfishness to unselfishness.

We go up from impurity to purity.

*There is only one
greatness—
inside greatness.
All outside greatness
is merely an
incidental reflection
of the inside.*

We go up from unhappiness to happiness.

We go up from weakness to strength.

We go up from low ideals to high ideals.

We go up from little vision to greater vision.

We go up from foolishness to wisdom.

We go up from fear to faith.

We go up from ignorance to understanding.

We go up by our own personal efforts. We go up by our own service, sacrifice, struggle and overcoming. We push out our own skyline. We rise above our own obstacles. We learn to see, hear, hold and understand.

We may become very great, very educated, rise very high, and yet not leave our home or business. We take our home or business right up with us! We make it a great home or great business. It becomes our throne room!

Come, let us grow greater. There is a throne for each of us.

Getting to the Top

"Getting to the top" is the world's pet delusion. There is no top. No matter how high we rise, we discover infinite distances above. The higher we rise, the better we see that life on this planet is the going up from the Finite to the Infinite.

The world says that to get greatness means to get great things. So the world is in the business of getting—getting great fortunes, great lands, great titles, great applause, great fame, and folderol. Soon the poor old world sees the emptiness of the inside, and wails, "All is vanity. I find no pleasure in them. Life is a failure." All outside life is a failure. Real life is in being something on the inside, not in getting things on the outside.

I weary of the world's accounts of "Getting to the Top" and "Forging to the Front." Too often they are the sordid story of a few scrambling over the heads of the weaker ones. Sometimes they are the story of one pig crowding the other pigs out of the trough!

How We Become Great

Christ Jesus was a great teacher. His mission was to educate and save humanity.

There came to him those two disciples who wanted to "get to the top." Those two sons of Zebedee wanted to have the greatest places in the new kingdom they imagined he would establish on earth.

They got very busy pursuing greatness, but I do not read that they were half so busy preparing for greatness. They even had their mother out promoting them.

"O, Master," said the mother, "grant that these my two sons may sit, the one on thy right hand, and the other on the left, in thy kingdom."

The Master looked with love and pity upon their unpreparedness. "Are ye able to drink of the cup?" Then he gave the only definition of greatness that can ever stand: "Whosoever will be great among you, let him be your minister; and whosoever will be chief among you, let him be your servant."

We cannot be "born great," nor "have greatness thrust upon" us. We must "achieve greatness" by developing it on the inside—developing the ability to minister and to serve.

We cannot buy a great arm. Our arm must become a great servant, and thus it becomes great.

We cannot buy a great character. It is earned in great moral service.

The First Step

Everyone's privilege and duty is to become great. And the joy of it is that the first step is always nearest at hand. We do not have to go chasing around the world to become great. It is a great stairway that leads from where our feet are now upward for an infinite number of steps.

We must take the first step now. Most of us want to take the hundredth step or the thousandth step now. We want to make some spectacular stride of a thousand steps at one leap. That is why we fall so hard when we miss our step.

We must go right back to our old place—into our kitchen or our school or our office and take the first step, solve the problem nearest at hand. We must make our old work luminous with a new devotion. We must battle up over every inch. And as fast as we solve and dissolve the difficulties and turn our burdens into blessings, we find love, the universal solvent, shining out of our lives. We find our spiritual influences going upward. So the winds of earth are born; they rush in from the cold lands to the warm upward currents. And so as our problems disappear and our life currents set upward, the world is drawn toward us with its problems. We find our kitchen or school or office becoming a new throne of power. We find the world around us rising up to call us blessed.

As we grow greater our troubles grow smaller, for we see them through greater eyes. We rise above them.

As we grow greater our opportunities grow greater. That is, we begin to see them. They are around us all the time, but we must get greater eyes to see them.

Generally speaking, the smaller our vision of our work, the more we admire what we have accomplished and "point with pride." The greater our vision, the more we see what is yet to be accomplished.

It was the young girl graduate who at commencement wondered how one small head could contain it all. In contrast, it was Newton after giving the world a new science who looked back over it and said, "I seem to have been only a boy playing on the seashore while the great ocean of truth lay all undiscovered before me." That great ocean is before us all.

The Widow's Mites

The Great Teacher pointed to the widow who cast her two mites into the treasury, and then to the rich men who had cast in much more. "This poor widow hath cast in more than they all. For all these have of their abundance cast in unto the offerings of God: but she of her poverty hath cast in all the living that she had."

Though the rich men had cast in more, yet it was only a part of their possessions. The widow cast in less, but it was all she had. The Master cared little about the amount of money in the treasury. That is not why we give. We give to become great. The widow had given all—had completely overcome her selfishness and fear of want.

Becoming great is overcoming our selfishness and fear. He that saves his life shall lose it, but he that loses his life for the advancement of the kingdom of happiness on earth shall find it great and glorified.

Our greatness therefore does not depend upon how much we give or upon what we do, whether peeling potatoes or ruling a nation, but upon the percentage of our output to our resources. Upon doing with our might what our hands find to do. Quit worrying about what you cannot get to do. Rejoice in doing the things you can get to do. And as you are faithful over a few things you will go up to be ruler over many.

CHAPTER SEVEN

Preparing to Live

THE PROBLEM OF "PREPAREDNESS" is the problem of preparing ourselves for life. All other kinds of "preparedness" fade into insignificance before this. The history of nations shows that their strength was not in the size of their armies and in the vastness of their population and wealth, but in the strength and ideals of the individual citizens.

As long as the nation was young and growing—as long as the people were struggling and overcoming—that nation was strong. It was "prepared."

But when the struggle stopped, the strength waned, for the strength came from the struggle. When the people became materially prosperous and surrendered to ease and indulgence, they became fat weaklings. Then they fell a prey to younger, hardier peoples.

Have we as a nation reached that period?

Many homes and communities have reached it.

Our Birthright

All over this country fathers and mothers who have struggled and have become strong men and women through their struggles are saying, "Our children shall have better chances than we had. We are living for our children. We are going to give them the best education our money can buy."

Then, forgetful how they became strong, they plan to take away from their children their birthright—their opportunity to become strong and "prepared"—through struggle and service and overcoming.

Many "advantages" are disadvantages. Giving a child a chance generally means getting out of his way. Many an orphan can be grateful that he was jolted from his life preserver and cruelly forced to sink or swim. Thus he learned to swim.

Some parents think they can buy an education—buy wisdom, strength and understanding, and give it to their children C.O.D.! They seem to think they will buy any brand they see—buy the local brand of education, or send off to New York or Paris for it. If they are rich enough, maybe they will have a private pipeline of education laid to their home. They are going to force this education into their children regularly until they get them full of education. They are going to get them fully inflated with education!

Get ready! There's going to be a "blow out." Those inflated children are going to have to run on "flat tires."

Parents cannot buy their children education. All they can do is to buy them some tools, perhaps, and open the gate and say, "Sic 'em!" The children must get it themselves.

A father and mother might as well say, "We will buy our children the strength we have earned in our arms and the wisdom we have acquired in a life of struggle." As well expect the athlete to give them his physical development he has earned in years of exercise. As well expect the musician to give them the technique he has acquired in years of practice. As well expect the scholar to give them the ability to think he has developed in years of study. As well expect Moses to give them his spiritual understanding acquired in a long life of prayer.

Parents can show the children the way, but each child must make the journey.

Here is a typical case.

The Story of "Gussie"

There was a factory town in the East. Not a pretty town, but just a great, dirty mill and a lot of little dirty houses around the mill. The workers lived in the little dirty houses and worked six days of the week in the big mill.

There was a little, old man who went about that mill, often saying, "I don't have any book learning like the rest of you." He was the man who owned the mill. He had made it with his own genius out of nothing. He had become rich and honored. Every man in the mill loved him like a father.

He had an idolatry for a book.

He also had a little pink son, whose name was F. Gustavus Adolphus. The little old man often said, "I'm going to give that boy the best education my money can buy."

He began to buy it. He began to polish and sandpaper Gussie from the minute the child could sit up in the cradle. When Gussie was old enough to export, he sent the boy to one of the greatest universities in the land. The fault was not with the university, not with Gussie, who was bright and capable.

The fault was with the little old man, who was so wise and great about everything else, and so foolish about his own son. In the blindness of his love he robbed his son of his birthright.

The birthright of every child is the opportunity of becoming great—of going up—of getting educated.

Gussie had no chance to serve. Everything was handed to him on a silver platter. Gussie went through that university about like a steer goes through a meat packinghouse.

You remember that after the steer matriculates—after he gets the grand bump, said steer does not have to do another thing. His education is all arranged for in advance and he merely rides through and receives it. He rides along from department to department until he is canned.

They "canned" Gussie. He had a man hired to study for him. He rode from department to department. They upholstered him, enameled him, manicured him, sugar-cured him, embalmed him. Finally Gussie was done and the paint was dry. He was a thing of beauty.

The Hero

Gussie came back home with his education in the baggage car. It was checked. The mill shut down on a week day, the first time in its history. The employees marched down to the depot, and when the young lord alighted, the factory band played, "See, the Conquering Hero Comes."

A few years later the mill shut down again on a week day. There was crepe hanging on the office door. Men and women stood weeping in the streets. The little old man had died.

When they opened the mill again, F. Gustavus Adolphus was at its head. He had inherited the entire plant. "F. Gustavus Adolphus, President."

Poor Gussie! He had never grown great enough to fill so great a place. In two years and seven months the mill was a wreck. The monument of a father's lifetime was wrecked in two years and seven months by the boy who had all the "advantages."

So the mill was shut down the third time on a week day. It looked as though it would never open. But it did open, and when it opened it had a new kind of boss. If I were to give the new boss a descriptive name, I would call him "Bill Whackem." He was an orphan. He had little chance. As a boy, he had a new black eye almost every day. But he seemed to fatten on bumps. Every time he was bumped he would swell up. How fast he grew! He became the most useful man in the community.

So when the courts were looking for someone big enough to take charge of the wrecked mill, they simply had to appoint Bill. It was Hon. William Whackem who put the wreckage together and made the wheels go round, and finally got the hungry town back to work.

Schools Give Us Tools

After that a good many people said it was the college that made a fool of Gussie. They said Bill succeeded so well because he never went to one of those "highbrow schools." I am sorry to say I thought that for awhile.

But now I see that Bill grew in spite of his handicaps. If he had possessed Gussie's equipment he might have accomplished vastly more.

Gussie was in the position of a man with a very good set of tools and no experience in using them. Bill was the man with the poor, homemade, crude tools, but with the energy, vision and strength developed by struggle.

The book and the college suffer at the hands of their friends who say to the book and the college, "Give us an education." They cannot do that. You cannot get an education from a book or a college any more than you can get to New York by reading a road map. You cannot get physical education by reading a book on gymnastics.

The book and the college show you the way, give you instruction and furnish you finer working tools. But the real education is the journey you make, the strength you develop, the service you perform with these instruments and tools.

Get the best tools you can. But remember diplomas and degrees are not an education, they are merely preparations. When you are through with the books, remember you are having a commencement, not an end-ment. You will discover with the passing years that life is just one series of greater commencements.

*You cannot get an
education from a
book or a college
any more than you
can get to New
York by reading
a road map.*

CHAPTER EIGHT

Helping Turkeys

AS A BOY, I once put some turkey eggs under the mother hen and waited day by day for them to hatch. And surely enough, one day the eggs began to crack and the little turkeys began to stick their heads out of the shells. Some of the little turkeys came out of the shells easily, but some of them stuck in the shells.

"Shell out, little turkeys, shell out," I urged, "for Thanksgiving is coming. Shell out!"

But they stuck to the shells.

"Helping" the Turkeys

"Little turkeys, I'll have to help you. I'll have to shell you by hand." So I picked the shells off. "Little turkeys, you will never know how fortunate you are. Ordinary turkeys do not have these advantages. Ordinary turkeys do not get shelled by hand."

Did I help them? I killed them, or stunted them. Not one of the turkeys was "right" that I helped. They were runts. Too many "advantages."

We must crack our own shells. We must overcome our own obstacles to develop our own powers.

A rich boy can succeed, but he has a poorer chance than a poor boy. The cards are against him. He must succeed in spite of his "advantages."

I am pleading for you to get a great arm, a great mind, a great character, for the joy of having a larger life. I am pleading with you to know the joy of overcoming and having the angels come and minister to you.

I am pleading with you to find happiness. All the world is seeking happiness, but so many are seeking it by rattling down instead of by shaking up.

The happiness is in going up—in developing a greater arm, a greater mind, a greater character.

Finding Happiness

Happiness is the joy of overcoming. It is the delight of an expanding consciousness. It is the cry of the eagle mounting upward. It is the proof that we are progressing.

We find happiness in our work, not outside of our work. If we cannot find happiness in our work, we have the wrong job. Find the work that fits your talents, and stop watching the clock and planning vacations.

Loving friends used to warn me against "breaking down." They scared me into "taking care" of myself. And I began taking such good care of myself and watching for symptoms that I became a physical wreck.

I saved myself by getting busier. I plunged into work I love. I found my joy in my work, not away from it, and the work refreshed me and rejuvenated me. Now I do two men's work, and have grown from a skinny, fretful, nervous wreck into a hearty, happy man. This has been a great surprise to my friends and a great disappointment to the family mortician. I am an editor in the daytime and a lecturer at night.

I edit all day and take a vacation lecturing at night. I lecture almost every day of the year—maybe two or three times some days—and then take a vacation by editing and writing. Thus every day is full of play and vacation and good times. The year is one round of joy, and I ought to pay people for the privilege of speaking and writing to them instead of them paying me!

If I did not like my work, of course, I would be carrying a terrible burden and would speedily collapse.

You see, I have no time now to break down. I have no time to think and worry about my body. Thus this old body behaves just beautifully and wags along like the tail follows the dog when I forget all about it.

I have never known a case of genuine "overwork."

I have never known of anyone killing himself by working. But I have known of multitudes killing themselves by taking vacations.

The people who think they are overworking are merely overworrying. This is one species of selfishness.

To worry is to doubt God.

To work at the things you love, or for those you love, is to turn work into play and duty into privilege. When we love our work, it is not work, it is life.

CHAPTER NINE

The Salvation of a Sucker

HOW LONG IT TAKES to learn some things! I think I was thirty-four years learning one sentence, "You can't get something for nothing." I still have not learned it. Every few days I stumble over it somewhere.

For that sentence utters one of the fundamentals of life that underlies every field of activity.

Reading and Knowing

All of us are Christopher Columbuses, discovering the same new-old continents of truth. That is the true happiness of life—discovering truth. We read things in a book and have a hazy idea of them. We hear the preacher utter truths and we say with little feeling, "Yes, that is so." We hear the great truths of life over and over and we are not excited. Truth never excites—

How long it takes to learn things! I think I was thirty-four years learning one sentence, "You can't get something for nothing."

it is falsehood that excites—until we discover it in our lives. Until we see it with our own eyes. Then there is a thrill. Then the old truth becomes a new blessing. Then the oldest, driest platitude crystallizes into a flashing jewel to delight and enrich our consciousness. This joy of discovery is the joy of living.

There is such a difference between reading a thing and knowing a thing. We could read a thousand descriptions of the sun and not know the sun as in one glimpse of it with our own eyes.

I used to stand in the row of blessed little rascals in school and read from McGuffey's celebrated literature, "If I play with fire, I will get my fingers burned."

I did not learn it. I wish I had learned by reading it that if I play with the fire I will get my fingers burned. I had to slap my hands upon hot stoves and coffeepots, and had to get many kinds of blisters in order to learn it.

Then I had to go around showing the blisters, boring my friends and taking up a collection of sympathy. "Look at my bad luck!" Fool!

You Can't Get Something for Nothing!

Yes, I was thirty-four years learning that one sentence: "You can't get something for nothing." It took me so long because I was naturally bright. It takes that kind of person longer than most. They are so smart you cannot teach them with a few bumps. They have to be pulverized.

I remember the first county fair I ever attended. Fellow sufferers, you may remember that at the county fair all the people sort out to their own departments. Even the "suckers"! Did you ever notice where they go?

I was in the middle of the suckers in five minutes. No one told me where they were. I didn't need to be told. I gravitated there. The barrel always shakes all of one size to one place.

At the entrance to the midway I met a gentleman. I know he was a gentleman because he said he was a gentleman. He had a small table he could move quickly. Whenever the climate became too sultry he would move to greener pastures. On that table were three little shells in a row, and there was a little pea under the middle shell. I saw it there, being naturally bright. I was the only naturally bright person around the table, hence the only one who knew under which shell the little round pea was hidden.

Even the gentleman running the game was fooled. He thought it was under the end shell and bet me money it was under the end shell. You see, this was not gambling, this was a sure thing. I had saved up my money for weeks to attend the fair. I bet it all on that middle shell. I felt bad. It seemed like robbing my father. And he seemed like a real nice old gentleman, and maybe he had a family to keep. But I would teach him not to "mess" with people like me, naturally bright.

But I needn't have felt bad. I did not rob father. Father cleaned me out of all I had in about five seconds.

I went over to the other side of the fairgrounds and sat down. That was all I had to do now—just go, sit down. I couldn't see the mermaid now or eat cotton candy or anything.

Sadly I thought it all over, but I did not get the right answer. I said the thing every fool does say when he gets bumped and fails to learn the lesson from the bump. I said, "Next time I shall be more careful."

When anyone says that—he is due for a return date.

My "Fool Drawer"

I grew older and people began to notice that I was naturally bright and therefore good picking. They began to let me in on the ground floor. Did anyone ever let you in on the ground floor? I never could stick. Whenever anyone let me in on the ground floor it seemed like I would always slide on through and land in the basement.

I used to have a drawer in my desk I called my "fool drawer." I kept my investments in it. I mean, the investments I did not have to lock up. I think you get the meaning of that—the investments no one wanted to steal. And whenever I would get unduly inflated I would open that drawer and "view the remains."

I had in that drawer the deed to my expensive corner lots. These lots were going to double next week. But they did not double—I doubled. They still exist on the blueprint and the metropolis on paper is yet a wide place in the road.

I had in that drawer my deed to my rubber plantation. Did you ever hear of a rubber plantation in Central America? That was mine. I had there my oil propositions. What a difference, I have learned, between an oil proposition and an oil well! The learning has been very expensive.

I used to wonder how I ever could spend my income. I do not wonder now. I wonder how I will make it.

I had in that drawer my "Everglade" farm. Did you ever hear of the "Everglades"? I have an alligator ranch there. It is below the frost-line, also below the water-line. I will sell it by the gallon.

I had also a bale of mining stock. I had stock in gold mines and silver mines. No one knows how much mining stock I have owned. No one could know while I kept that drawer shut. As I looked over my gold and silver mine stock, I often noticed that it was printed in green. I used to wonder why they printed it in green—wonder if they wanted it to harmonize with me! And I would realize I had so much to live for—the dividends. I have been so near the dividends I could smell them but I never got them.

Being "Selected"

Why go farther? I am not half finished confessing. Each bump only increased my faith that the next ship would be mine.

I was also greatly interested in companies where I put in one dollar and got back a dollar or two of bonds and a dollar or two of stock. That was doubling and trebling my money over night. An old banker once said to me, "Why don't you invest in something that will pay you five or six per cent, and get it?"

I pitied his lack of vision. Bankers were such "tightwads." They had no imagination! Nothing interested me that did not offer fifty or a hundred per cent—then. Give me the five per cent now!

By the time I was thirty-four I was a rich man in worthless paper. It would have been better for me if I had thrown all my savings into the bottom of the sea.

Then I got a confidential letter from a friend of our family I had never met. His name was Thomas and he lived in St. Louis. He wrote me in extreme confidence, "You have been selected."

Were you ever selected? If you were, then you know the thrill that pulsed my manly chest as I read that letter from this man who said he was a friend of our family. "You have been selected because you are a prominent citizen and have a large influence in your community. You are a natural leader and everyone looks up to you."

He knew me! He was the only man who did know me. So I took the cork clear under.

"Because of your tremendous influence you have been selected to go in with us in the inner circle and get a thousand per cent dividends."

Did you get that? I hope you did. I did not! But I took a night train for St. Louis. I was afraid someone might beat me there if I waited until the next day. I sat up all night in a day coach to save money for Tom, the friend of our family. But I see now I need not have hurried so. They would have waited a month with the sheep-shears ready.

O, I am so glad I went to St. Louis. Being naturally bright, I could not learn it at home, back in Ohio. I had to go to St. Louis to Tom Cleage's business and pay him eleven thousand dollars to corner the wheat market of the world. That is all I paid him. I could not borrow any more. I joined what he called a "pool." I know it must have been a pool, for I know I fell in and got soaked!

That bump made me think. My fever began to reduce. I got the thirty-third degree in financial suckerdom for only eleven thousand dollars.

I have always regarded Tom as one of my great school teachers. I have always regarded the eleven thousand as the finest investment I had made up to that time, for I got the most out of it. I do not feel hard toward "goldbrick" men and "blue sky" vendors. I sometimes feel that we should endow them. How else can we save a sucker? You cannot tell him anything, because he is naturally bright and knows better. You simply have to cheat him until he bleeds.

It is worth eleven thousand dollars every day to know that one sentence, "You can not get something for nothing." Life just begins to get juicy when you know it. Today when I open a newspaper and see a big ad, "Grasp a Fortune Now!" I will not do it! I stop my subscription to that paper. I simply will not take a paper with that ad in it, for I have graduated from that class.

I will not grasp a fortune now. Try me, I dare you! Bring a fortune and put it in front of me. I will not grasp it. Get away, it is a coffeepot!

Today when someone offers me much more than the legal rate of interest I know he is no friend of our family.

If he offers me a hundred per cent I call for the police!

Today when I get a confidential letter that starts out, "You have been selected—" I never read farther than the word "selected." I select the waste basket.

The law of compensation is never suspended. You can't get something for nothing. If you do not learn it, you will have to be "selected." There is no other way for you, because you are naturally bright. When you get a letter, "You have been selected to receive a thousand per cent dividends," it means you have been selected because you look like the biggest sucker on the local landscape.

CHAPTER TEN

Getting in Tune

DID YOU EVER HEAR a young preacher, just captured, just out of a factory? Did you ever hear him preach his first sermon? I wish you had heard mine. I had a call. At least, I thought I had a call. I think now I was "short-circuited." The "brethren" discussed it and told me I had been "selected." Maybe this was a local call, not long distance.

My First Sermon

They gave me six weeks in which to get ready. But I made the mistake I am trying to warn you against. Instead of going to the one book where I might have gotten a sermon—the book of my experience, I went to the books in my father's library. "As the poet Shakespeare has so beautifully said," and then I took a chunk of Shakespeare and nailed it on page five of my sermon.

"List to the poet Tennyson." Come here, Lord Alfred. So I welded these fragments from the books together with my own native genius. I worked that sermon up into the most beautiful splurges and spasms. I bedecked it with metaphors and semaphores. I filled it with emotional peaks, both wet and dry.

I committed it all to memory, and then went to a lady who taught me to gesture. I nailed the most beautiful gestures into almost every page.

I got up before a mirror for six weeks, day by day, and said the sermon out loud. It got so it would run itself. I could have gone to sleep and that sermon would not have hesitated.

Then came the grand day. The boy wonder stood forth and before his large and enthusiastic audience delivered that maiden sermon more grandly than ever to a mirror. Every gesture went off according to the blueprint. I cried on page fourteen! I never knew it was in me. But I certainly got it all out that day!

Then I did another fine thing, I sat down. I wish now I had done that earlier. I wish now I had sat down before I got up. I was the last man out of the church—and I hurried. But they beat me out—all nine of them. When I went out the door, an old man said as he jiggled the key in the door to hurry me, "Don't feel bad, I've heard worse than that. You're all right, but you don't know anything yet."

I cried all the way home. If he had plunged a dagger into me he would not have hurt me as much. It has taken some years to learn that the old man was right. I had wonderful truth in that sermon. No sermon ever had greater truth, but I had not lived it. The old man meant I did not know my own sermon.

Theory and Practice

The world is full of theorists and dreamers who have worthy visions but are not able to translate them into practical realities. They go around with their heads in the clouds, looking upward, and half the time their feet are in the flower beds or trampling upon their fellow men they dream of helping. Their ideas must be forged into usefulness upon the anvil of experience.

Many of the most brilliant theorists have been the greatest failures in practice.

There are a thousand people who can tell you what the problems are to every one person who can give you a practical solution.

I used to have respect amounting to reverence for great readers and "book people." I used to know a man who could tell in what book almost anything you could think of was discussed, and perhaps the page. He was a walking library index. In my childhood I thought he was the greatest man in the world.

He was a remarkable man—a great reader and with a memory that retained it all. That man could recite chapters and volumes. He could give you almost any date. He could finish almost any quotation. His conversation was largely made up of classical quotations.

But he was one of the most helpless men I have ever seen in practical life. He seemed unable to think and reason for himself. He could quote a page of John Locke, but somehow the page never supplied the one sentence needed for the occasion. The man was a misfit on earth. He was just as likely to put the gravy in his coffee and the gasoline in the fire. He seemed never to have digested any of the things in his memory. Since I have grown up, I always think of that man as an intellectual cold storage plant.

After the Bible, the greatest book is the textbook of the University of Hard Knocks, the Book of Human Experience—the "sermons in stones" and the "books in running brooks." Most fortunate is he who has learned to read understandingly from it.

Tuning the Strings

Each person in the world is different, reading a different page in the Book of Human Experience. Each has a different fight to make and a different burden to carry. Each one of us has more trouble than anybody else!

I know there are chapters of heroism in the lives of you older ones. You have cried yourselves to sleep and walked the floor when you could not sleep.

Many of you were bumped today or yesterday, or maybe years ago, and the wound has not healed. You think it never will heal.

And you young people are not very interested in this because down in your hearts you are asking, "What is this all about? What is that man talking about? I haven't had these problems and I'm not going to have them, either!"

You are going to be bumped. You are going to cry yourselves to sleep. You are going to walk the floor when you cannot sleep. Some of you are going to know the keen sorrow of having the one you trust most betray you. Maybe, betray you with a kiss. You will go through your Gethsemane. You will see your dearest plans wrecked. You will see all that seems to make life livable lost out of your horizon. You will say, "God, let me die. I have nothing more to live for."

For all lives have about the same elements. Your life is going to be about like other lives.

And you are going to learn the wonderful lesson through the years, the bumps and the tears, that all these things somehow are necessary to promote our education.

These bumps and hard knocks do not break the

violin—they tune the strings.

These bumps and tragedies and Waterloos draw the strings of the soul tighter and tighter, nearer and nearer to God's great concert pitch. The discords fade from our lives and the music divine and harmonies celestial come from the same old strings that had been sending forth the noise and discord.

Thus we know that our education is progressing, as the evil and unworthy go out of our lives and as peace, harmony, happiness, love and understanding come into our lives.

That is getting in tune.

That is growing up.

CHAPTER ELEVEN

The Price of Memories

WHAT A PRICE WE PAY for what we know! I laugh as I look backward—and weep and rejoice.

I was not born with a silver spoon in my mouth, although it is quite evident that I could have handled a pretty good-sized spoon. Because my father was a country preacher, we had tin spoons. We never had to tie a red string around our spoons when we loaned them for the ladies' aid society oyster supper. We always got our spoons back. No one ever traded with us by mistake.

Do you remember the first money you ever earned? I do. I walked several miles into the country and worked all day on a farm. That night I was proud when that farmer patted me on the head and said, "You are the best boy to work, I ever saw." Then the

*I was not born with
a silver spoon in my
mouth, although it
is quite evident
that I could have
handled a pretty
good-sized spoon.*

cheerful old miser put a nickel in my blistered hand. That nickel looked bigger than any money I have since handled.

But I was years learning it is much easier to make money than to handle it, hence the tale that follows.

Last Day of School

I was sixteen years old and I became a school teacher. Sweet sixteen—which means green sixteen. But remember again, only green things grow. There is hope for green things. I didn't tell them my age, but I bid for the local school teaching job. I was several dollars the lowest bidder. They said, "Anybody can teach kids." That is why I was a teacher.

I had never studied education, but I had whittled out three rules that I thought would work. My first rule was, "Make them study." My second, "Make them recite." My third and most important rule was, "Get your money."

We ended the school year with an "exhibition." People came that day from all over the area. They were so glad our school was closing for the summer they all turned out to make it a success. They brought great baskets of food and we had a feast—piles of fried chicken and forty kinds of pie.

Then we had a "doings" and everyone performed. We executed a lot of literature that day. Execute is probably the best word to describe what happened to literature that day. I can close my eyes and still see it. I can see my students coming forward to speak their "pieces." I hardly knew them and they hardly knew me, for we were "dressed up."

I can see "The Soldier of the Legion lay dying in Algiers." We had him die again that day, and he had a lingering end as we executed him. I can see "The boy stood on the burning deck, whence all but he had fled." I can see "Mary's little lamb" come skipping over the stage. I see the tow-headed patriot in "Give me liberty or give me death." I feel now that if Patrick Henry had been present, he would have said, "Give me death."

There came a breathless hush as I came forward at the end to say farewell. It was customary to cry. I wanted to yell. Tomorrow I would get my money! I had a speech I had been saying over and over until it would say itself. But somehow when I got up before that "last day of school" audience and opened my mouth, nothing came out. It came out of my eyes. Tears rolled down my cheeks until I could hear them spatter on my six-dollar suit.

And my students wept as their dear teacher said farewell. Parents wept. It was a teary time. I only said, "Weep not for me, dear friends, I am going away, but I am coming back." I thought to cheer them up, but they wept the more.

The Joyous Wad

The next day I received my money. I had it all in one joyous wad—$240. I was going home with head high and aircastles even higher. But I never got home with the money. Talk about the fool and his money and you get very personal.

For on the way home I met Deacon K, and he borrowed it all. Deacon K was "such a good man" and a "pillar of the church." I used to wonder though why he didn't take a pillow to church. He signed a note for the $240, but I really thought a note was not necessary, such was my confidence in the deacon.

For years I kept a faded, tear-spattered, yellow note for $240 as a souvenir of my first schoolteaching. Deacon K has gone from earth. He has gone to his eternal reward. I scarcely know whether to look up or down as I say that. He never left any forwarding address.

I was paid thousands in experience for that first schoolteaching, but I paid all the money I got from it—two hundred and forty dollars to learn one thing I could not learn from books. I learned that it takes less wisdom to make money than it does to intelligently handle it afterwards. Incidentally, I learned it may be safer to do business with a first class sinner than with a second class saint.

• CHAPTER TWELVE •

Looking Backward— and Forward

YEARS AFTER I LEFT HOME, I went back to my hometown to speak. I stood upon the same platform where twenty-one years before I had stood to deliver my graduating oration.

After the speech, I went back to the little hotel and sat up alone in my room half the night reliving the past. I used to think anyone who could live in that hotel was a superior order of being. But now I realized that anyone who could go on living in any hotel has a superior order of determination.

I held thanksgiving services that night. I could see better. I had found a truer perspective of life. Did you ever sit alone with a picture of your classmates taken twenty-one years before? It is a memorable experience.

The Brilliant and Gifted

A class of brilliant and gifted young people went out to take charge of the world. They were so glad the world had waited so long on them. They were so willing to take charge of the world. They were going to be presidents and senators and authors and scientists and geniuses.

There was one boy in the class who was not naturally bright. It was not the one you may be thinking of! No, it was Jim Lambert. He had no brilliant career in view. He was dull and seemed to lack intellect. He was "promoted" into the senior class. We all felt a little sorry for Jim.

As commencement day approached, a group of seniors took Jim aside and broke the news to him that he was going to graduate, but we were not going to let him speak. He couldn't make a speech that would do credit to such a brilliant class. They hid Jim on the stage behind the oleander commencement night.

The girl who was to become the author became an operator at the telephone company, and had become absolutely indispensable to the community. The girl who was to become the poet became the superintendent of the post office. The boy who was going to Congress was raising the best corn in the county, and his wife was speaker of the house.

Most of them were doing very well—even Jim Lambert. Jim had become the head of one of the big manufacturing plants of the South. The committee that took him aside to inform him he could not speak at commencement, would now have to wait in line before a frosted door marked, "Mr. Lambert, Private." They would have to send up their business cards, and the watchdog who guards the door would tell them, "Keep it short, he's busy!" before they could break any news to him today.

They hung a picture of Mr. Lambert in the high school at the last alumni meeting. They hung it on the wall near where the oleander stood that night.

Roll Call

Hours passed, and as I sat in that hotel room, I was lost in that school picture and the twenty-one years. There were fifty-four young people in that picture.

Out of that fifty-four, one had gone to a pulpit, one had gone to Congress and one had gone to prison. Some had gone to brilliant success and some had gone down to sad failure. Some had found happiness and some had found unhappiness. It seemed as though almost every note on the keyboard of human possibility had been struck by the one class of fifty-four.

When that picture was taken, the oldest person

was not more than eighteen, yet most of them seemed already to have decided their destinies. The twenty-one years that followed had not changed their courses.

The only changes had come where God had been allowed into a life to lift it up, or where Mammon had entered to pull it down. And I saw better that the foolish dreams of success faded before the natural unfolding of talents, which is the real success. I saw better that "the boy is father to the man."

The boy who skimmed over his work in school was skimming over his work as a man. The boy who went to the bottom of things in school was going to the bottom of things in manhood.

Jim Lambert had merely followed the call of talents unseen in him twenty-one years before.

The lazy boy became a "tired" man. The industrious boy became an industrious man. The sporty boy became a sporty man. The domineering egotist boy became the domineering egotist man.

The boy who traded knives with me and beat me—how I used to envy him! Why could he always get the better of me? Well, he went on trading knives and getting the better of people. Now, twenty-one years afterwards, he was doing time in prison for forgery. He was now called a bad man. Twenty-one years ago when he did the same things on a smaller scale they called him smart.

The boy who didn't mix with the other boys, who didn't whisper, who never got into trouble, who always had his hair combed, and said, "If you please," used to upset me. He was the teacher's model boy. All the mothers of the community used to say to their own reprobate offspring, "Why can't you be like Harry? He'll be President of the United States some day, and you'll be in jail." But Model Harry sat around all his life being a model. I believe the dictionary defines a model as a small imitation of the real thing. Harry certainly was a successful model. He became a seedy, sleepy, helpless relic at forty. He was "nice and polite" because he didn't have the energy to be anything else. The boys with hustle and energy, who occasionally needed bumping—and who got it—were the ones who really grew.

I have said little about the girls of the school. At that age I didn't pay much attention to them. I regarded them as in the way. But I naturally thought of Clarice, our social butterfly of the class who won first place in the local beauty contest. Clarice went right on remaining in the social spotlight, primping and flirting. She outshone all the rest. But it seemed like she was all outshine and no in-shine. She mistook popularity for success. The boys voted for her but did not marry her. Most of the girls who shone with less social luster became the happy women of the community.

The Boy I Had Envied

Frank was the boy I had envied. He had everything—a fine home, a loving father, plenty of money, opportunity and a great career awaiting him. And he was bright and lovable and talented. Everyone said Frank would make his mark in the world and make the town proud of him.

After commencement, Frank and most of the other seniors left for college or to pursue exciting careers.

But the week after commencement I had to go into a printing office, roll up my sleeves and go to work to earn my daily bread. Seemed like it took so much bread!

Many a time as I plugged along I would think of Frank and wonder why some people had all the good things and I had all the hard things.

How easy it is to see as you look backward. But how hard it is to see when you look forward.

Twenty-one years later when I returned, I asked, "Where is he?" We went out to the cemetery, where I stood at a grave and read on the headstone, "Frank."

I heard the story of a tragedy—the tragedy of modern unpreparedness. It was the story of the boy who had every opportunity, but who had all the struggle taken out of his life. He never followed his career, never developed any strength. He disappointed hopes, spent a fortune, broke his father's heart, shocked the community, and finally ended his wasted life by his own hand.

Why Ben Hur Won

Do you remember the story of Ben Hur?

The Jewish boy is torn from his home in disgrace. He is hauled into court and tried for a crime he never committed. Ben Hur did not get a fair trial.

Then they condemn him. They lead him away to the galleys. They chain him to the bench and to the oar. Day after day he pulls on the oar. Day after day he writhes under the sting of the lash. Years of the cruel injustice pass. Ben Hur is the helpless victim of a mocking fate.

That seems to be your life and my life. Wherever we work, we seem so often like slaves bound to the oar and pulling under the sting of the lash of necessity. Life seems one futureless round of drudgery. We wonder why. We often look across the street and see someone who lives a happier life. That one is chained to no oar. See what an exciting life they have. Why must we pull on the oar?

How blind we are! We can only see our own oar. We cannot see that they, too, pull on the oar and feel the lash. Most likely they are looking back at us and

*I thanked God
for parents who
believed in the
gospel of struggle,
and for the
circumstances that
compelled it.*

envying us. For while we envy others, others are envying us.

But look at the chariot race in Antioch. See the thousands in the stands. See Messala, the haughty Roman, and see Ben Hur from the galleys in the other chariot pitted against him. Down the course dash these twin thunderbolts. The thousands hold their breath.

"Who will win?"

"The man with the stronger forearms," they whisper.

There comes the crucial moment in the race. See the man with the stronger forearms. They are bands of steel that swell in the forearms of Ben Hur. They swing those flying Arabians into the inner ring. Ben Hur wins the race! Where got the slave those huge forearms? From the galleys!

Had Ben Hur never pulled on the oar, he never could have won the chariot race.

Sooner or later you and I will learn that Providence makes no mistakes in the bookkeeping. As we pull on the oar, so often lashed by grim necessity, every honest effort is laid up at compound interest in the bank account of strength. Sooner or later the time comes when we need every ounce. Sooner or later our chariot race is on—when we win the victory, strike the deciding blow, stand while those around us fall—

and it is won with the forearms earned in the galleys of life by pulling on the oar.

That is why I thanked God as I stood at the grave of my classmate. I thanked God for parents who believed in the gospel of struggle, and for the circumstances that compelled it.

I am not an example of success.

But I am a very grateful student in the freshman class of The University of Hard Knocks.

CHAPTER THIRTEEN

The Defeats That Are Victories

How Often We Say, "I wish I had a million!" Perhaps it is a blessing that we have not the million. Perhaps it would make us lazy, selfish and unhappy. Perhaps we would go around giving it to other people to make them lazy, selfish and unhappy.

Oh, the problem is not how to get money, but how to get rid of money with the least injury to the race!

Perhaps getting the million would completely spoil us. Look at the wildcat and then look at the house cat. The wildcat supports itself and the house cat has its million. So the house cat has to be pampered daily and doctored by specialists.

If the burden were lifted from most of us we would become a wreck. Necessity is the ballast in our life voyage.

When you hear a good speaker and you note the ease and power of his words, do you think of the years of struggle he spent in preparing? Do you think of the times that person tried to speak when he failed and left in disgrace, mortified and broken-hearted? Through it all came the discipline, experience and grim resolve that made him succeed.

When you hear the musician and note the ease and grace of the performance, do you think of the years of struggle and overcoming necessary to produce that finesse and grace? That is the story of the actor, the author and every other person of achievement.

Do you note that people grow more in lean years than in fat years? Failures and business problems are not calamities, but blessings in disguise. People go to the devil with full pockets; they turn to God when hunger hits them.

You have to shoot many men's eyes out before they can see. You have to crack their heads before they can think, knock them down before they can stand, break their hearts before they can sing, and bankrupt them before they can be rich.

Do you remember that they had to lock John Bunyan in Bedford jail before he would write his immortal "Pilgrim's Progress"? It may be that some of us will have to go to jail to do our best work.

Do you remember that one musician became deaf

before he wrote the music the world will always hear? Do you remember that one author became blind before writing "Paradise Lost," a book the world will always read?

Do you remember that Saul of Tarsus would have never been remembered had he lived the life of luxury planned for him? He had to be blinded before he could see the way to real success. He had to be scourged and fettered to become the Apostle to the Gentiles. What throne rooms are some prisons! And what prisons are some throne rooms!

Do you not see all around you that success is ever the phoenix rising from the ashes of defeat?

Then, when you stand in the row of graduates on commencement day with your diplomas in your hands, and when your relatives and friends say, "Success to you!" I shall take your hand and say, "Defeat to you! And struggles to you! And bumps to you!"

For that is the only way to say, "Success to you!"

O University of Hard Knocks, we learn to love you more with each passing year. We learn that you are cruel only to be kind. We learn that you are saving us from ourselves. But O, how most of us must be bumped to see this!

O University of Hard Knocks, we learn to love you more with each passing year. We learn that you are cruel only to be kind. We learn that you are saving us from ourselves. But O, how most of us must be bumped to see this!